CHILDREN OF THE PAST

ARCHAEOLOGY AND THE LIVES OF KIDS

LOIS MINER HUEY

M MILLBROOK PRESS • MINNEAPOLIS

In memory of our parents, who gave us lots of love —L.M.H.

Front cover: Stenciled handprints decorate the walls of Cueva de las Manos (Cave of Hands) in Río Pinturas, Argentina. The cave art was made between nine thousand and thirteen thousand years ago.

Back cover: Archeologists carefully uncover skeletal remains in Jamestown, Virginia. They can learn more about how colonial children and adults lived by studying artifacts discovered at the site.

Special thanks to the content consultants who provided feedback on portions of this book. Chapter 3: Kathryn Kamp, Earl D. Strong Professor of Social Studies, Department of Anthropology, Grinnell College; chapter 4: Lissa Tenuta, Department of Research & Collections, Historic St. Mary's City.

Millbrook Press
A division of Lerner Publishing Group, Inc.
241 First Avenue North
Minneapolis, MN 55401 USA

For reading levels and more information, look up this title at www.lernerbooks.com.

Main body text set in Avenir LT Pro 45 Book 11.5/15. Typeface provided by Linotype AG.

Library of Congress Cataloging-in-Publication Data

Names: Huey, Lois Miner, author.
Title: Children of the past : archaeology and the lives of kids / Lois Miner Huey.
Description: Minneapolis : Millbrook Press, [2017] | Audience: Grades 4 to 6. | Includes
   bibliographical references and index.
Identifiers: LCCN 2016019761 (print) | LCCN 2016033625 (ebook) |
   ISBN 9781512413168 (library bound : alkaline paper) | ISBN 9781512428438 (eb pdf)
Subjects: LCSH: Children, Prehistoric—Juvenile literature. | Children—History—
   Juvenile literature. | Social archaeology—Juvenile literature.
Classification: LCC GN799.C38 H84 2017 (print) | LCC GN799.C38 (ebook) | DDC
   305.2309/01—dc23

LC record available at https://lccn.loc.gov/2016019761

Manufactured in the United States of America
1-39775-21313-5/27/2016

CONTENTS

INTRODUCTION

Did you know that kids in the past were a lot like you? They played, made things, and did tasks around the house. In fact, if you were to meet one of these children from the past, it probably wouldn't be long before you'd be playing together and sharing stories about your favorite activities.

But children in the past also were different. For example, a lot of your learning happens in school. In the past, kids mostly learned at home. And kids back then played, but they also worked from a young age. They learned to draw pictures, make stone tools, chase birds away from crops, create clay pots, and more. They learned what they needed to know to live in their times. Their labor was important to their families and also to the larger group they belonged to.

So how do we get to know these kids from the past? We have some written records, but not very many. In Jamestown, the first successful English settlement in what later became the United States, people didn't even bother recording the birth of the first baby there! We have other clues, though. Archaeologists can find out about children by studying the stuff they left behind. It's interesting to think about what these kids looked like or what they wore. But it's even more exciting to learn what they *did*. From children playing in prehistoric caves to hardworking teens in an early colony to courageous kids escaping slavery, let's explore the lives of some children from the past.

Archaeologists found this piece of a bottle at the Fort Mose site near Saint Augustine, Florida.

Archaeologist Mary Anna Richardson carefully works to reveal an artifact in Jamestown, Virginia.

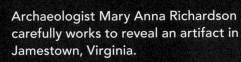

A student archaeologist digs at an excavation site at Fort Mose near Saint Augustine, Florida.

Thousands of years ago, people in many parts of the world made projectile points and other tools out of stone. These flint tools come from North Africa and were made between six thousand and nine thousand years ago.

CHAPTER 1
CAVE-ROAMING KIDS

Western Europe
Twenty Thousand Years Ago (18,000 BCE)

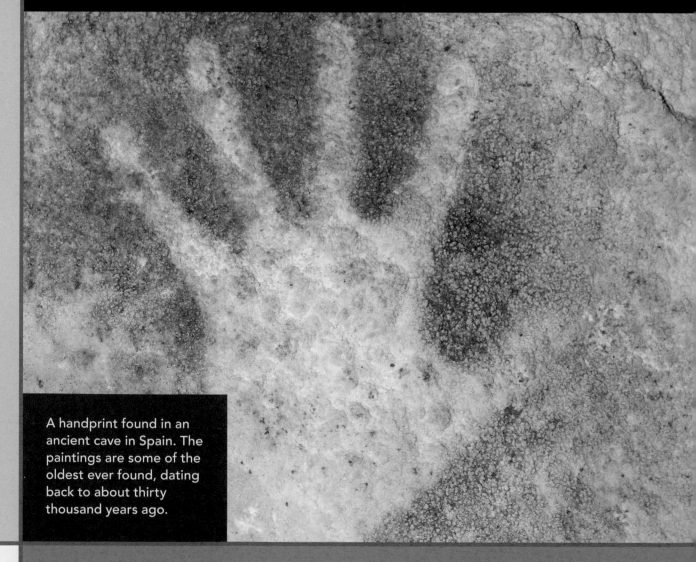

A handprint found in an ancient cave in Spain. The paintings are some of the oldest ever found, dating back to about thirty thousand years ago.

North Atlantic Ocean

EUROPEAN CONTINENT

N

Your father swings you up onto his shoulder. You laugh and hang on to his thick hair while you kick your feet on his chest. Your kicking makes him laugh. You look over at your mother, who carries your baby brother. Together you walk toward a cave near your family's campsite.

When you enter the cave, you call out so the echo of your voice rolls back to you. Giggling, you slide down off your father's shoulders and run a little way ahead. You know where you're going. What you might not notice are the footprints you leave in soft clay on the cave floor.

When you reach your destination, you reach up and touch a small handprint outlined on the rock. It's yours—put there when you were a baby. Now it's Brother's turn.

Your father holds a small rock hollowed out in the middle to make a bowl. It is filled with paint that you watched him make this morning. It's a mixture of charcoal, powdered red rock, and water. Your mother holds Brother's hand against the cave wall and nods at you to help her hold it still and steady. Brother coos as he feels the cool stone. Your father carefully sucks some of the paint into a hollow bird bone and then blows through the bone to spray the paint in an outline around the baby's hand. You laugh as some red color lands on your hand too.

You climb back onto your father's shoulders, giving a quick tug on his beard as you clamber up. As you ride out of the cave, you drag your fingers along the ceiling above you, leaving long trails of lines in the soft clay there. When your father notices what you're doing, he starts weaving from side to side as he walks. Your patterns become wavy. What fun!

For years, archaeologists, historians, and others have admired ancient cave art found in countries such as Spain and France. Radiocarbon dating of charcoal from the art shows that most were created between ten thousand and thirty thousand years ago. What does it mean? Some scientists think these paintings have to do with religion. Others believe the art shows that early people needed to create. One thing they *didn't* expect was that children had much to do with the art. If children were involved at all, they thought, it was only as part of special ceremonies when boys symbolically became adults and joined the men as hunters.

RADIOCARBON DATING

Radiocarbon is an element found in certain natural materials such as wood, bone, and shell. Radiocarbon breaks down at a steady rate. Scientists measure this rate to determine when the material was alive. This helps establish the date of a sample and is a valuable tool for archaeologists.

A scientist takes a bone sample for radiocarbon dating.

A painting in one of France's Lascaux caves shows a group of animals. These images may be up to twenty thousand years old.

However, many historians are beginning to think that we may be taking cave art a little too seriously. Experts still believe that the finest animal paintings were done by adults and that there may have been ceremonies connected to this work. But many other images and paintings were not made with such skill. Archaeologists have come to believe that kids made a lot of this art and that the handprints and finger fluting don't have deep meaning but were just for fun. These ideas shine new light on the lives of cave kids.

HANDPRINTS

Handprints in European caves have two main forms. Some are outlines or stencils, as described in the story starting this chapter. Others are full handprints that seem to have been made by putting paint on the hand and then pressing it against the wall. Stencils show not just hands but also arms, feet, and even whole human bodies. The fully painted prints found so far are almost all of hands only.

LIVING IN CAVES? WELL, NOT QUITE

You've probably heard the term *caveman* or *cave people*. But archaeologists have learned that most early Europeans didn't live *in* caves. Caves were cold, damp, and slippery—hardly good places to live. Some families built shelters near cave entrances, but most lived in animal skin tents and wooden huts. They took these shelters with them as they moved around to search for food.

This cave in Spain contains paintings of wild animals and human hands that date back more than eleven thousand years.

Measuring the handprints has revealed that most were from youngsters. In one study, out of 201 stenciled handprints measured, 186 were from people sixteen and younger—all the way down to infants. The smallest prints from babies had to have been made with the help of adults or teenagers. The midsize prints were from kids two to eleven years old. The largest were from males aged twelve to sixteen. Although we can't explain why, boys made most of the handprints. These handprints may represent a desire to make a mark—to leave a sign saying, "I was here!" That's still a common impulse. Most handprints were probably "fun art" as opposed to the fine animal paintings decorating cave walls. Some prints seem to have fingers "missing." Archaeologists realize these were created with fingers folded down and are not the work of injured people as they once thought. Doesn't this seem as if it's something a kid might do?

Archaeologists have also studied footprints from these people. Almost all the footprints found in hardened clay on European cave floors were left by children. Although there are adult footprints, 90 percent are children's! Because adults are heavier, they would have left more prints if a lot of them were

Prehistoric handprints in a Spanish cave

in the caves with kids. Since so many footprints are from children, that tells us that kids roamed around inside caves without adult supervision. Some footprints are from children as young as three years old. Most, however, were from nine- to fifteen-year-olds. Older kids probably took younger ones with them to play in the caves, do some artwork, and just hang out away from the grown-ups. More kids went into caves than adults.

In addition, there were simply a lot of kids. Studies suggest that out of a group of thirty-five people at that time, twenty-four of them would have been teenagers or younger. More kids, so more prints. That also helps explain the greater number of young people's footprints in the caves.

A child left this footprint in a French cave more than ten thousand years ago.

FINGER FLUTING

Another design found in caves is finger fluting, also called finger tracing. Archaeologists have found these marks on cave ceilings and walls in Europe, as well as in Australia and New Guinea. They've been a mystery for years. Why did ancient people make these marks? What did they mean?

Archaeologists do think they know *how* the marks were made: by holding the hand's three middle fingers together and dragging them through soft surfaces in caves. The marks were preserved when these surfaces eventually hardened. Archaeologists have measured the widths of the closed fingers of modern-day children and adults and compared them with cave flutes. Based on these measurements, they've concluded that most flutes are the work of children. Finger widths also tell us whether the fluter was a male or female, because female finger widths are smaller.

One famous fluted surface is the ceiling of a French cave. Most fluting there and beyond was done by children aged two to five. Adults must have held them up so they could reach the ceiling. Those holding the kids walked around while the children dragged their fingers in a swirling or wavy pattern.

Finger flutes are often found in remote areas of caves where access is difficult. These spaces were too tiny for adults. But kids were smaller, more flexible, and more adventurous. They went deeper into the dark caves. In the same French cave with the famous fluted ceiling, two young children and a teenager explored the inner chambers. Here they fluted and drew pictures. The children returned to the main cave to add more flute marks to the work of adults who were busy painting pictures of animals.

In that same cave, one young girl liked to mark high on the wall, above the adult art. Her work is in several of the cave's chambers. The adult or teenager carrying her must have been amused as she insisted that her marks be higher than the others!

Cave carvings made with fingers or with tools are found all over the world. These come from Australia and are about twenty thousand years old.

In another cave, about eight or nine people fluted, including a baby, two young children, and five or six older kids. In yet another cave, all the fluting seems to have been done by three people: a child, a woman, and a man. The woman seems to have been carrying the child on her right hip. The child's smaller fluting appears to the right of the marks the woman made. The man drew semicircles and circles. In at least two places, he seems to have jumped up, leaving his reaching fingerprints behind.

"I WAS HERE!"

Modern archaeologists believe that children from thousands of years ago played in and helped decorate the famous art caves of Europe with their drawings, handprints, and finger flutes. They left their marks for us to see, study, and wonder about. Their activities show that families valued their kids and let them explore, giving them the chance to roam in and out of the caves on their own. They enjoyed this freedom and sometimes used it to amuse themselves and their friends by leaving evidence of their presence there.

The caves may have been places where important ceremonies took place to please hunting spirits, initiate boys into adulthood, and fulfill an urge to create art. But they also echoed with giggles, whispers, and laughter as children explored, marked, and enjoyed them.

CHAPTER 2
HUNTER-GATHERER KIDS

Europe
Eight Thousand Years Ago (6000 BCE)

This site in Scotland was the home of prehistoric people more than four thousand years ago. At the center is the hearth, where tools were made and food was prepared.

Approximate Landmass in 7,000 BCE

North Atlantic Ocean

○ Ancient landmass

○ Current landmass

EUROPEAN CONTINENT

N

Excited and a little nervous, you and your sister join a group around the hearth. A man hands each of you a rock. Disappointed, you see that it's not a very good rock—not one that will produce good stone tools. It's a rock for a beginner—which is what you are. You are even more disappointed when you're told to stay in the back of the ring of workers around the man who is teaching the class. More experienced students get to sit at the front. You and your sister sit up on your knees so you can see better. Then you settle back down to begin work.

In one hand, you hold the rock you were given. In the other, you grip a stone that just fits in your palm, which you also had been given. You pound this stone down on the first rock. Ouch! You hit your finger. Your sister giggles. You can see that she's making progress—two chips from her rock already lie on the ground in front of her. You frown and go back to work. Someday, you'll be good at this, but it's going to take lots of practice.

STONE TOOLS

For thousands of years, men, women, and children across Europe and beyond used stone tools. Some were weapons. But they were also much more. In fact, daily activities depended on these tools. Hunter-gatherers roamed across the land hunting animals and gathering plants for food. They stayed for a while in one place and then moved on, following the animals or looking for warmer places to live.

One of the most important stone tools these people made was the projectile point. These points were sharp stone tips made from stone and attached to wooden shafts, creating spears. Hunters hurled—or projected—these spears at animals (and sometimes humans). Projectile points were used for hunting thousands of years before humans invented the bow and arrow. Other stone tools were knives, axes, clubs, and chunks of stone used as hammers (called hammer stones).

Prehistoric flint tools from Italy

Of course, hunter-gatherer kids and adults didn't go out and just find projectile points and knives lying around. These tools had to be made by hand. Making them well required a lot of training and practice. In the past, historians thought that boys made most stone tools. However, modern-day archaeologists realize that girls too learned these skills. Although girls didn't participate in hunting, they needed stone tools to cut plant roots and leaves, remove skin from dead animals, and slice meat for meals.

STONE TOOL TECHNIQUE

Many archaeologists have closely studied the making of stone tools. They have learned that it can take twenty-five hits with a hammer stone to trim a rock down to a slimmer shape. If that isn't working, the maker throws the rock away and begins again. If it is working, the maker takes more careful hits to make the rock into a triangle. Then the maker switches to what is called pressure flaking. A pointed wooden or bone tool is pressed against the stone and pressed down, so tiny fragments flake off the edge to make it sharp.

This is a lot of work, but experts can make a point like this in minutes. It takes beginners—like kids—much longer to learn how to produce a usable point.

Archaeologists aren't completely sure how kids learned to make tools, and it varied from place to place. Did they attend a class? Did they learn individually from adults? Or did they simply watch skilled toolmakers and then try the techniques on their own?

In some places, at least, children attended classes. The story that starts this chapter was based on evidence from an ancient French site called Solvieux. Archaeologists there studied stone chips that had been buried in the ground thousands of years ago. The people who chipped away at the rocks are called knappers. Archaeologists saw that the chipping techniques of knappers sitting farthest from the center hearth were the roughest. Beginners used too much force, stopped their strikes too soon, and threw down rocks without finishing the work. Those closest to the teacher and the hearth were more skilled, and their work was more precise.

This prehistoric stone hammer comes from a site in northern Italy.

At Solvieux, archaeologists mapped where stone chips fell to the ground as students worked. Then they fitted these chips back onto the rocks they had come from. (Imagine what a jigsaw puzzle that was!) By doing this, they could trace the progress of one knapper as he or she moved around the area.

Near the edge of the site, this student began working on a low-quality rock. Archaeologists found most of the chips knocked off the rock in this area. But then a problem must have developed, because the next fragment of the rock was found about 9 feet (3 meters) away, closer to the center. Perhaps the student went there to ask for help from a more experienced knapper. An expert removed a piece of the rock, which landed on the ground there. The kid then moved about 4 feet (1.2 m) away. There, archaeologists found the next piece struck off the rock. But it came off badly. He or she walked away from that bad piece and about 2 feet (0.6 m) farther on struck the rock again, and this time, it split in half. That was it. The student threw both halves down, showing how frustrating it was to try to make a projectile point. It's not an easy skill to learn. But the kid deserves credit for trying so hard and not giving up until forced to do so!

JOBS FOR KIDS

Along with learning to make stone tools, kids did other jobs in hunter-gatherer societies. For example, they went with adults to quarries where they helped choose good rock for making tools (and not-so-good rock for beginners like them to practice with).

In Europe this rock is flint. It splits along certain lines when it's hit correctly. This quality makes it excellent for toolmaking. (People in North America made stone tools too. But the type of rock found there isn't the true flint found in Europe. It is called chert.)

Prehistoric people made tools out of various materials. These tools are between four thousand and seven thousand years old and are made from deer antlers. The tools were found in a flint mine in Great Britain.

HOW DID HUNTER-GATHERERS COOK THEIR FOOD?

We know that early hunter-gatherers used rocks to make tools, weapons, and hearths. Guess what else they did with rocks? They cooked their food with them! Women put small rocks—about the size of a plum—into the hearth among the flames. Once these rocks (which kids probably collected) were red hot, the women fished them out with sticks and dropped them into nearby containers made of tree bark or animal skin filled with water and food. The rocks caused the water to become hot. As the stones cooled, they were pulled out and replaced with hot ones until the food was cooked. Later, hunter-gatherers made stone pots using soft rock called steatite (STEE-uh-tite), or soapstone. They hollowed out the rock, put in water and food, and placed this cooking pot right on the stone hearth.

Prehistoric people may have used this steatite bowl for cooking or holding food. It comes from southern Italy.

Kids also waded into streams looking for hammer stones. They searched the streambeds for these rocks, which knappers used to pound good pieces of flint (or chert) into shape.

Another job kids did was gathering rocks to build hearths. Then, because fires were essential for cooking and for warmth, boys and girls gathered wood to burn in those hearths. The longer the group stayed in the same place, the farther they had to go to find wood. When collecting wood became too difficult, the group would move to a new spot.

While wandering in forests or fields, kids also collected antlers shed by deer. These were one source of the bone tools that projectile point makers used for finishing points. And kids were sent to collect sticky sap from trees and other plants to use as glue for holding the points on the spears. Girls also helped their mothers cook animal fat and make glue from it. Children were involved in the making of stone tools from beginning to end.

Besides making tools and picking up stones, kids helped gather wild foods growing around their camps. What kinds of food did they gather and eat? We find out by examining their poop!

POOP

That's right. Archaeologists have found and studied ancient human bowel movements, called coprolites, or scat. If you're wondering, they don't smell when they're found. But they do stink when broken apart—a smell that has been hidden for thousands of years! Some are found in caves where they had dried out. Other coprolites have been found frozen in the Arctic.

Inside ancient coprolites, archaeologists have found acorns, walnuts, pecans, and other nuts. Seeds from grass, berries, onions, grapes, and flowers are present. The coprolites also contain animal parts: bits of mice, pack rats, fish, lizards, snails, bird eggs—and insects like grasshoppers, caterpillars, crickets, and beetles. You might not think bugs sound too tasty, but they are very nutritious.

More rarely, scientists have found bits of antelope, bison, and elk in ancient coprolites. Hunters would have hit large animals like these with their projectile points. Men and boys also fished, and they captured smaller animals like rabbits in snares. Still, the plants gathered by women and girls were probably the core of these people's diet. Studies have shown that the more successful the men were in providing meat, the less plant gathering the women and girls did. If there was a shortage of meat, the group ate more plants, berries, seeds, and nuts.

An archaeologist studies a coprolite from more than ten thousand years ago. This specimen was found in the northwestern United States.

PART OF THE GROUP

Hunter-gatherer kids stayed busy learning many skills they would need as adults. They also learned through games and contests. Who could find the best rocks for making projectile points? Who could throw a spear the farthest? Maybe you can imagine them laughing and shouting as they competed. And they learned to work together too—gathering food and supplies, and exploring their world. In their free time, boys and girls roamed about the camp and nearby fields and woods, enjoying freedom away from supervising adults. Most important, though, these children participated directly in the everyday work of adults. They were part of the group and made contributions important to everyone.

This kind of life went on for thousands of years. Gradually, at different times and in different parts of the world, people began to move around less and grow their own food. This was a huge change in human history.

CHAPTER 3
FARMER KIDS

North America
One Thousand Years Ago (1000 CE)

A modern-day re-creation of a Huron village in Ontario, Canada

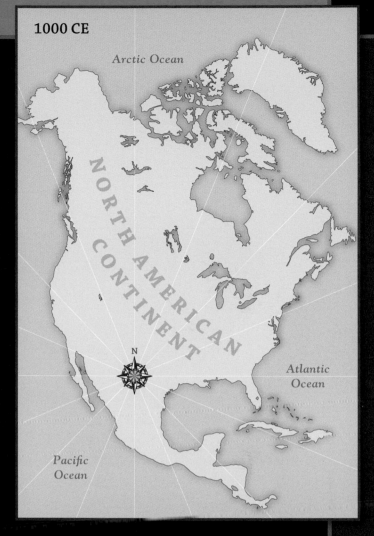

Arctic Ocean

NORTH AMERICAN CONTINENT

N

Atlantic Ocean

Pacific Ocean

You and the other children follow the old woman toward the farm fields. You look back at the homes in your village and see the smoke coming from holes in the roofs. Your parents, along with your mother's sisters and their husbands, live together in these elm bark-covered homes. Smiling at the sight, you turn to look at the growing crops. These are the Three Sisters: corn, beans, and squash. All the crops are doing well. They thrive here in the northeastern climate. The corn is tall, and the beans have wound tendrils up the cornstalks. Squash has spread out in the shade of the corn. Over the years, the men from your village have removed trees and bushes to clear these fields. Women and children plant the crops here and then protect them from troublesome creatures like crows and rats.

You sigh. Instead of running around the field chasing off pesky animals, you'd rather make clay pots. When you were younger, you started out making simple pots pinched out of the clay. But you've grown more skilled. You love mixing the soft clay with stone to make it stronger. Then you roll this mixture into coils. You use this process to form good, useful pots. You're still learning to make pots. But you're getting better and better at it.

FINGERPRINTS

An archaeologist looks at a clay pot fragment and sees a fingerprint. This pot's maker left her signature behind, even if she didn't actually sign it. Her mark is unmistakable and unique. Could a child have made it?

Fingerprints show on a piece of American Indian pottery. This pot was made by an adult member of the Pueblo people, who live in the southwestern United States.

Scientists and archaeologists have developed a method that helps reveal the age and gender of the person who made a fingerprint. Fingerprint ridges grow wider as a person gets older. So by measuring the ridges' width, archaeologists can judge the person's age. They determine gender based on the size of the prints themselves, as female fingers are narrower than male fingers. For example, archaeologists working at ancient sites settled by Pueblo American Indians (in the southwestern United States, far from the northeastern villages of the Huron people) have studied thousand-year-old fingerprints left on clay artifacts. These prints have revealed that children as young as four were making childlike figurines with four legs. They may have represented common animals like dogs or deer. Wider fingerprint ridges on other pieces show that by the age of twelve, girls were making large pots with skill.

American Indian women and girls used clay pots to cook, store, and serve food. Early in life, girls learned how to form and decorate these pots. First,

HOW DO SCIENTISTS MEASURE FINGERPRINT RIDGES?

Fingerprints are fully developed in babies at seven months of age. The prints increase in size as the child grows older. The same number of ridges remain, but they get wider, and so do the spaces between them. At about the age of eighteen, fingerprint growth stops. Using a measuring tool called a caliper *(below),* researchers measure ridge widths by beginning at the edge of a ridge and going across it to the beginning of the next ridge. This is done under a bright light and a magnifying glass.

they made pots so small that archaeologists think they were used as toys. Later, girls progressed to making full-sized, useful objects. Since clay pots sometimes broke, women had to work to keep up with the demand for them.

Were American Indian boys involved in this crafting of clay? Yes, when they were young—probably less than seven. From infancy, both boys and girls spent most of their time with their mothers and saw them do a wide variety of daily tasks. As kids got older, they were able to help. They collected clay and mixed in stones, and then watched mom, big sisters, aunts, and older women make pots. Both boys and girls also took care of crops in the field, fetched water, and did other helpful tasks.

When boys were old enough, they joined the men to learn hunting skills. But boys had already learned a lot about what women and girls did. This likely helped them understand how everyone in the group contributed—and how they were going to help too by bringing in meat to cook in those strong clay pots!

DECORATED POTS

Most of the pots children made were plain—but not all of them. A Canadian archaeologist named Patricia Smith studied over a thousand decorated pots made by both young people and adults from the Huron people. These American Indians lived in the northeastern part of North

LEARNER POTS

At many prehistoric farming sites, archaeologists have found fragments of pots and also sometimes whole clay pots. Those that adults created are finely made and decorated with different types of designs. But archaeologists also find small pots that are less skillfully made.

For a long time, these little pots mystified scientists. Who made them? How were they used? Eventually, most experts concluded that these were children's practice pots. Young students learned to make them with adults' help, by watching closely and then trying it themselves.

Experts think a child may have crafted this small bowl. It comes from the southern United States and was probably made by a member of the Caddoan Mississippian group of American Indians.

America. She learned that quite a few kids' pots were decorated. The pots this archaeologist examined were made during three different time periods between the late thirteenth century and the seventeenth century. She compared designs on juvenile pots with those on adult pots. Three types of designs were found on the kids' pots: horizontal lines (back and forth), vertical lines (up and down), and geometric shapes (such as circles and triangles). Smith counted the number of times each was used on both kids' and adult pots.

Horizontal decorations were the most common design on the oldest pots made by adults. Most American Indian households had three generations of women living there: daughters, mothers, and older women in the family. Mothers were busy gathering plants, cooking, cleaning the home, and caring for babies. So older women probably did most of the teaching. They taught pot making and likely encouraged pupils to use the traditional horizontal designs. But kids often didn't do that. Instead, they made the vertical designs they preferred. Kids weren't copying adult designs. Instead, they were creating designs that they chose.

Geometric designs also found on juvenile pots but seldom on adult ones. Imagine a girl drawing a geometric shape like a circle and showing it to her friends. They then did it too, but maybe with circles of different sizes or by placing them on different places on the pot. And the copying—and innovation—went on from there. The same independence and creativity in decoration was found at another Canadian site. Kids at the Calvert site (in what became Ontario) also made small crude pots. Over half of those found had no decoration. But the other half did—and they were not decorated with the same designs used by adults there. These kids too were decorating their pots with designs that pleased them. Can you imagine them giggling and laughing as they competed to come up with something unique?

This pot was made by a member of the Iroquois peoples, American Indians from the Northeastern United States.

HELPING OUT

Farming kids did many of the same daily tasks that hunter-gatherer kids did. They collected wood for fires, helped care for younger children, helped collect clay and mix it for pot making, and assisted in preparing meat and corn for the pot that always simmered over a fire. They enjoyed freedom from adults when they took trips to the forests and fields. When the wood supply dwindled and crops had worn out the soil, they helped pack up their belongings, move the village to another location, and rebuilt their home. Farming kids still hunted and gathered along with the adults, but they also planted, cared for, and harvested crops. Like children before them, they contributed to the well-being of the whole community, something that must have made them feel important and proud.

CHAPTER 4
COLONIAL KIDS

Jamestown, Virginia, North America
Four Hundred Years Ago (1600s CE)

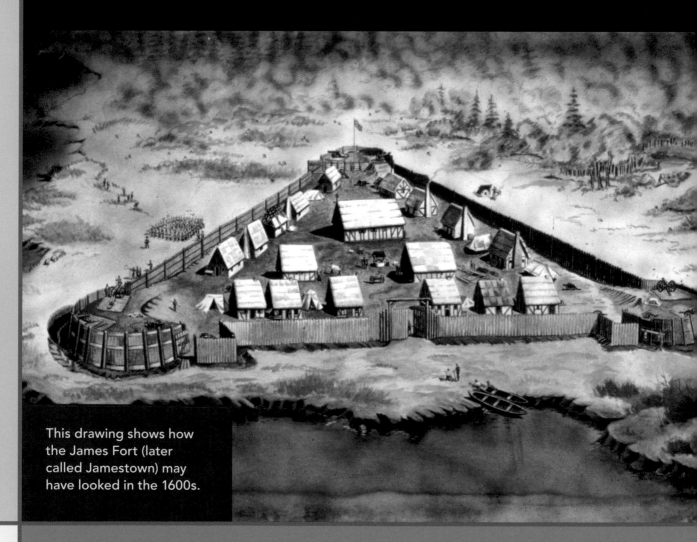

This drawing shows how the James Fort (later called Jamestown) may have looked in the 1600s.

You stride down the path through James Fort to the glasshouse where men are making glass objects. The Virginia Company paid your way from England to the Jamestown settlement in North America in 1608. Since then, you've been helping the glassmakers. You're fourteen, so you can work hard, but you don't have the skills of the older German and Polish glassmakers who also came here. Instead of making glass, you helped make the glasshouse itself. You hauled boulders to build the furnaces. You cut wood to make the building's frame. Now your jobs are to chop wood to feed the furnaces and to collect sand to use in glassmaking.

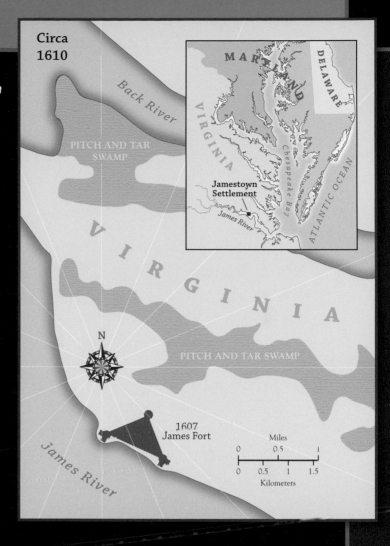

As you draw near, you hear the roar of the furnaces and the quarreling voices of the men. You sigh. These workers came here to make glass vases and other goods to be sent back to England. But over time, glassmaking has almost stopped. You used to feel proud of this blossoming industry in a new country, but it's just not working. Life is so hard in Jamestown. Some people search for gold and other valuable resources, as directed by the company. Others struggle to grow crops and hunt animals. Having enough food is a big problem, since many European crops don't grow well here. Jamestown residents sometimes buy food from neighboring American Indians, but when those people are short on food, trading stops. The settlers have to slap hungry mosquitoes, try to stay healthy, avoid poisonous snakes, and avoid conflict with the American Indians in the area— all while trying to get used to the heat. It's worn everyone down. The chances of a successful glassmaking industry here don't look good. Not good at all.

In 1607 the Virginia Company—a business group in London—sent colonists to North America. The company hoped settlers would find gold and also make products like glass to sell in Europe. Over the centuries, Europeans had cut down many trees. They began using coal in their furnaces instead of wood. But wood-stoked fires were better for glassmaking. Finding a new supply of trees in America was exciting. The colonists had other ideas too. They hoped they could make silk in North America along with wine, dyes, medicine, and more. But the colonists' early efforts did not succeed. By 1610 it looked as though the settlers would have to abandon Jamestown. Gold was nowhere to be found, and glassmaking had stopped. Hundreds of people had died, mostly from illness. The remaining colonists decided to head back to England. But while traveling down the James River to the ocean, they met a new supply ship coming from England. The supplies renewed their hope, and they turned back to try again. By 1616 Jamestown had become the first successful English settlement in North America.

LIFE IN JAMESTOWN

Teenage boys were part of Jamestown from the beginning. They were among the early colonists. They came as either servants for the wealthier men or as apprentices to the Virginia Company. Many more children and teenagers followed when Jamestown finally began to flourish after 1610. Children in the colony worked hard along with their parents. They swept floors, delivered messages, tended crops, gathered wood for fires, watched younger children, and more.

The children of this settlement played too. But archaeologists working at Jamestown have uncovered only a few toys. Most of the toys and games from this time were probably made of organic material like wood or cloth and have rotted away in the ground. A few metal toys have survived. Among them are tiny lead horses with arched necks and short tails. These horses probably had riders once, but they have disappeared—along with the horses' legs! Archaeologists at Jamestown

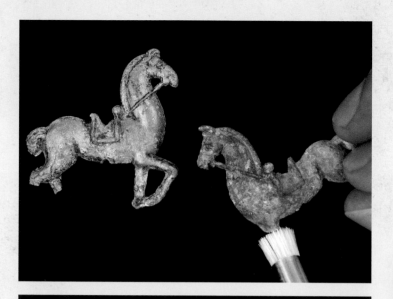

Kids at Jamestown likely played with these miniature toy horses made of lead.

Age has changed the color of this toy windmill. When the plaything was new, it was probably copper-colored.

also found a tiny 1-inch high (2.5-centimeter) brass house with a steep roof. Historians think it was probably a toy windmill that once had spinning blades. Kids could pull on a string to set the windmill's blades spinning.

Archaeologists at Jamestown have also found other items that belonged to children. One was a slate used for practicing writing. Another was a brass thimble with a piece of paper stuffed inside. They believe it belonged to a little girl who was learning to sew. The thimble she had was too large for her tiny fingers, so someone used paper to make it fit. In addition, archaeologists found a baby's shoe in a well. Perhaps the baby was being held near the well when the shoe fell off the child's foot. Or the baby may have pulled it off and thrown it—as babies sometimes do! Imagine the shocked reaction of the adult and the giggles of the baby as the shoe disappeared down into the deep well. For experts, this was an exciting find because it told historians that babies were in Jamestown. Babies were not recorded in the colony's documents. Even the first child born in Jamestown wasn't mentioned. So artifacts like the shoe help add to what we know about life in Jamestown.

AMERICAN INDIANS NEAR JAMESTOWN

Powhatan, father of Pocahontas, was the most powerful chief in the area around Jamestown. He united many different tribes under his control, including the Appomattuck, Kecoughtan, Moraughtacund, and Warraskoyack. All spoke related languages and in modern times are known as Algonquin tribes.

This 1624 illustration shows Powhatan, the father of Pocahontas.

Ætatis suæ 21. Aº.1616.

This painting of Pocahontas is from 1616. It depicts her wearing English-style clothes.

One youngster who spent time at Jamestown was Pocahontas. She was the daughter of the most powerful American Indian leader in the area. Her father worked with the English settlers for a long time, partly because he appreciated trading with them and partly because he thought they might help him fend off his enemies in the area. Meanwhile, Pocahontas was fascinated with these strangers and visited Jamestown often, bringing food to the hungry settlers. She also joined children in playing games. In 1612 one person who lived in the fort wrote a report to the company in London. In his report, the writer said that Pocahontas was an active young girl of about "eleven or twelve years" and that she turned cartwheels in the clearing in front of the fort. Other children followed her lead. They raced around, chasing one another and laughing until they were breathless.

LIFE WITH THE AMERICAN INDIANS

Henry Spelman expected to be one of those Jamestown children. But that is not what happened. In October 1609, after months of sailing from England, he stepped off a ship onto the American shore—only to find out two weeks later that he wasn't going to live in Jamestown after all. So what was in Henry's future? It turned out that Captain John Smith, who was in charge of the settlement, had sold Henry to a group of local American Indians.

How could Smith do this? Smith had the right to make this arrangement because the Virginia Company—which Smith worked for—had paid for Henry to sail to the New World. In return for that payment, Henry became indentured to the company, which gave it control over his life until he could pay it back. Smith had an idea for how Henry could repay his debt. He wanted the fourteen-year-old to learn American Indian ways and languages to help the English communicate with their neighbors. But he hadn't told Henry about this plan.

Henry soon adapted to his new life, however. Little Powhatan—the son of the local American Indian leader—welcomed him to his village, which was also called Powhatan. Henry later wrote in a journal that Little

A modern-day re-creation of a Powhatan village

Powhatan "made very much of me givinge me such thinges as he had to winn me to live with him." (You might think Henry's spelling looks a little odd. That's because he was writing in the days when spelling was not as standardized as it is now. So Henry wrote words according to how they sounded to him.)

Over the next year or so, Henry lived in several different American Indian villages, where he learned about the lives, languages, and cultures of Jamestown's American Indian neighbors. All the people Henry lived with were called Powhatan by the English, after the name of their leader. Sometimes these people and villages were also called Powhatan's Confederacy. The villages where Henry stayed each had round, roomy houses made of wooden frames covered with reed mats or bark. People sat on woven mats on the floor. In the roof's center, a hole let out smoke from the fire that cooked food and warmed the house.

Henry probably continued to wear his English clothes, although sometimes he might have slipped on deerskin moccasins like those the

American Indians around him wore. Henry kept his English hairstyle too. The men in the villages where Henry stayed let their hair grow long on the left side and cut it very short on the right side of their heads. That way the hair didn't get in the way when they drew back a bow to release an arrow. And unlike the English, most men in these villages plucked their facial hair. No beards for them!

Henry hunted deer with the men, just as the boys from the villages did. He also joined them clearing fields for planting. The main crop was corn. Henry watched carefully as the women and girls of the village dug holes in the field and placed four or five kernels of corn in each hole, along with two beans. When the crops were ripe, the women did the work of harvesting the corn, drying it in the sun, removing kernels from the cobs, and storing the corn. Henry ate stews made of corn mixed with meat like venison, both new foods to him.

Along with tasting new foods, Henry took part in the village's games. In one game played by women and boys, the object was to kick a ball to make goals. Men played a similar game with a smaller ball. Players dropped the ball and hit it with the tops of their feet. The man who knocked the ball the farthest won.

Henry danced with people in his village too. In one dance he described, men and women stood in a circle around a man holding a rattle and playing a flute. Henry and the others in the circle stamped their feet on the ground and shook their heads to the beat, probably rotating around the musician in the circle's center. The dancers sang, Henry wrote, but "Drums and Trumpetts they have none."

Archaeologists believe these stone pieces found at Jamestown were used either for making food or for crafting arrowpoints.

HENRY SPELMAN'S LATER HISTORY

After Henry Spelman returned to living with the Jamestown settlers, he continued to work as an interpreter. In 1622 an American Indian leader named Opechancanough, who was a half brother of Powhatan, tried to force the English out of the region. Opechancanough's men killed more than three hundred settlers, but Spelman survived. Warfare continued, however, and in 1623, he volunteered to go north from Jamestown with a group of men to trade for food, as the settlers needed supplies badly. But he and his men were attacked, and Spelman was killed. He was twenty-eight years old.

Eventually, the English bought Henry back from the American Indians he'd lived with. Henry had grown to enjoy the American Indian way of life. He served for years as an interpreter between the two groups, doing his part to persuade the American Indians and the Jamestown settlers to get along.

SUCCESS AND TRAGEDY

The English came to Jamestown expecting to find gold, create industries, build communities, and grow food. The American Indians who already lived in the area made stone tools, grew abundant crops, and built many villages. The two groups lived differently but found that working together could help them all. The English needed help as they struggled to grow crops in this strange environment. American Indians could provide that help. In return, they welcomed metals that the colonists brought, such as copper and iron. Similarly, American Indians were experts at trapping animals, and Jamestown settlers wanted furs to send back to England. A brisk trade took place.

All of this worked until American Indian leaders realized the Jamestown settlers were not planning to leave. Instead, they were spreading out and claiming even more land. Settlers left Jamestown and settled up and down local rivers, building forts and farms, and going farther and farther into American Indian territory. After the supply ships arrived in 1610, a new English governor sent soldiers on raids into American Indian villages, killing men, women, and children to establish control over these groups and the land they lived on. These raids launched a series of conflicts sometimes called the Anglo-Powhatan Wars. After the First Anglo-Powhatan War (ca. 1610–1614), smaller raids and clashes continued until the Second Anglo-Powhatan War (1622–1632) erupted after Powhatan's death. After the Third Anglo-Powhatan War (1644–1646), English leaders and members of the Powhatan Confederacy signed a treaty that established lasting English dominance over most of the area.

These wars were devastating for the American Indian communities around Jamestown. In addition, the settlers brought diseases American Indians never had encountered: smallpox, measles, mumps, and other deadly illnesses. American Indians died in large numbers because they had no immunity to these diseases.

CHAPTER 5

KIDS OF FORT MOSE

Florida
250 Years Ago (1700s CE)

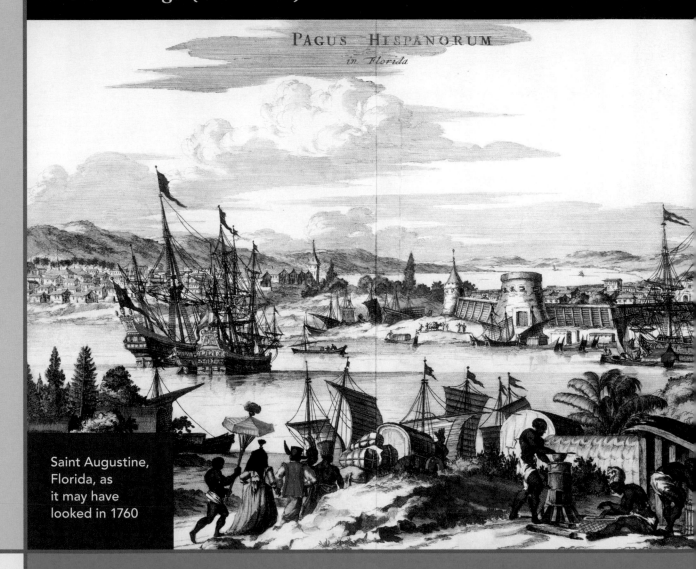

PAGUS HISPANORUM
in Florida

Saint Augustine, Florida, as it may have looked in 1760

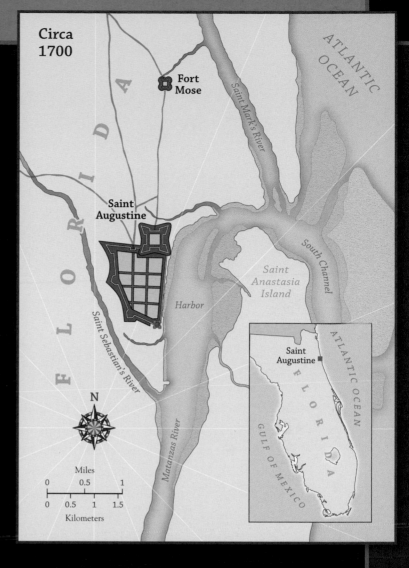

You sit in a canoe, peering into the dark night. Your parents sit behind you, and American Indians paddle the boat through the swamp. All of you are silent. As African slaves brought forcibly to the New World, you and your family are escaping your captivity in South Carolina and traveling south into Spanish Florida.

A branch snaps, and you freeze. Are you being followed? Your mother clutches you, but the guides stay calm, so you sit up straight and try to be brave. You have heard that you will be welcomed as free people in Saint Augustine, the Spanish city that is your destination. You will have to adopt Roman Catholicism—the religion of the Spanish settlers. And you'll pledge to help defend the Spanish from enemies. These are small prices to pay for freedom. Slaves have escaped this way for many years. It's your turn. As the sun rises, you see a large fort through the mist. It's Saint Augustine. You've made it!

In 1686 the Spanish—who were enemies of the English at the time—began spreading the word that they would offer sanctuary and freedom to slaves who came to Florida. As far as historians know, the first known group of escaped slaves arrived in 1687. It included eight men, two women, and a baby. In 1693 the Spanish passed a law saying that all slaves who escaped to Florida would be given liberty. This passage to freedom—sometimes called the Southern Underground Railroad—lasted until the British claimed Florida in 1763. Enslaved people also fled

SLAVERY IN NORTH AMERICA

Slavery in North America began in 1619 when English settlers began buying captives brought from West Africa to do forced labor on their farms (sometimes called plantations) and in their homes. Slave traders loaded tens of thousands of African captives onto ships carrying them to the Caribbean and North America. Slavery was legal in parts of what is now the United States for more than three hundred years, and many slaves faced horrific treatment at the hands of traders and owners. Some of these enslaved people risked their lives to escape from their white owners. Of those who successfully escaped, some established settlements in the local swamps or lived with American Indians nearby. Others fled to the parts of Florida that were controlled by Spain. These areas were outside the British colonies.

Enslaved people working on a North American tobacco plantation in 1725

to the North. Those who were able to reach the North were relatively safe in states that had already outlawed slavery, beginning with Vermont in 1777. Later, however, a law called the Fugitive Slave Act of 1850 said that all escaped slaves had to be returned to their owners, no matter what state they had reached. So people had to go even farther north, into Canada, where slavery had been outlawed.

FORT MOSE

Saint Augustine was a major city in Florida, and many of the people who escaped enslavement headed toward this settlement. In fact, so many slaves fled to Saint Augustine that by 1738, the Spanish settlers in Saint Augustine encouraged these then free people to move a few miles north to live together in a separate settlement that also was a fort. This arrangement pleased the free blacks who wanted to have their own home. In addition, the Spanish were happy to have settlers living along the northern frontier of their territory. From that position, they could help fight enemies of the Spanish. This was Fort Mose (moh-ZAY), the first legal settlement for free black people in what became the United States.

In 1740 British forces attacked Fort Mose. Some of the fort's inhabitants helped the Spanish fight back against the British and win the battle. However, Fort Mose and its town were destroyed during the fighting. Fort Mose's residents relocated to Saint Augustine itself. Twelve years later, the Spanish urged them to build a new free black settlement near the original fort. From there they could help defend Saint Augustine again, if needed. The inhabitants once again called the settlement Fort Mose. According to Spanish records, twenty-two families lived there, including fifteen children (seven boys and eight girls). The kids of Fort Mose ran about the town, chatting with one another in various languages. (Before being forced into slavery, the people who came to Fort Mose had lived in different areas of Africa and the Caribbean.) Kids were a big part of life and work in this busy place.

What was the second Fort Mose like? Archaeologists found the settlement's site on what is now a small island. (They found where the first Fort Mose was too, but it is underwater and hard to reach.) The new fort had three sides made of earth covered with sticky clay. On top of the walls, cannons and swivel guns sat ready for battle. Surrounding these three sides of the fort was a ditch called a moat, designed to protect the fort against enemies. The moat was filled with prickly pear cactus. Enemies didn't want to go through all that to reach the walls!

The fourth side of the fort was open toward the river, which was another barrier against enemies. A small wooden Roman Catholic chapel sat not far from the river. A Roman Catholic priest visited Fort Mose often. Children attended the religious services along with their families.

A watchtower close to the fort's center provided views in all directions. Some of the older kids may have been assigned to take a turn watching for enemies. The rest of the time, the children went out to the fields surrounding the settlement and pulled weeds or ran around chasing birds away from the precious crops. They also joined the adults in fishing, helping bring home food for the family table.

Coming back home, some children entered rectangular houses like those they had known on the British farms where they had once been

HELPERS AND GUIDES ALONG THE PATH TO FREEDOM

American Indians including the Creek, Cherokee, and Yemassee helped people who were escaping slavery and going to Fort Mose. These American Indians were sometimes guides through the swamps and forests around Fort Mose, as described in the story that opens this chapter. And some families who were fleeing slavery lived in American Indian villages for a time before they reached Fort Mose.

enslaved. But unlike those homes, the roofs were thatched with palm leaves. Others lived in oval-shaped buildings made of palm thatch similar to those their families had known in Africa. Inside their homes, kids probably waited—sometimes impatiently!—for their mothers to feed them. Archaeologists found seeds and other food remains in this area that included corn, figs, squash, melons, beans, oranges, and wild berries. Kids at the fort probably helped gather these foods, along with hunting and catching animals including turtles and rabbits. Historians don't know for sure if there was a school at the fort, but they believe the priest probably did his best to teach the children whenever he was there.

The number of clay pots found at the fort suggests that American Indians from groups like the Creek, Cherokee, and Yemassee also came to Fort Mose. They had probably married escaping slaves and joined them in Florida. The clay pots made by these people were large, the types used for food storage. But the presence of European-made ceramic pots also suggests that people used those for eating. In addition, archaeologists found pewter spoons that were used for eating stews cooked in the pots. Wine bottles show that adults drank wine with meals. Imagine the children of Fort Mose sitting inside their various homes, eating food they'd helped to grow, gather, or catch and dipping small metal spoons into their tasty meals. Yum!

Bottles found by archaeologists at Fort Mose

In and around this settlement, archaeologists found buttons, buckles, a brass finger ring, a Saint Christopher medal, and rosary beads. These last two are Catholic symbols. That isn't too surprising, since the escaped slaves had agreed to adopt the Catholic religion. What surprised the experts, however, was the discovery of small blue beads. In West Africa, where many of the former slaves had originally come from, such blue beads were considered powerful symbols that protected people from sickness or evil spirits. Sometimes West African parents placed these beads on their children as a way to ensure

Saint Christopher medals have been found at many different archeological sites. Catholic travelers have long carried these medals for protection. According to legend, Christopher lived in the 200s BCE. He is frequently depicted carrying a child, believed to be an embodiment of Jesus, across a body of water.

good luck. Experts believe that they were probably doing the same thing at Fort Mose. These beads show that while the newest residents of Florida may have officially converted to the Roman Catholic religion, they still practiced their old traditions too.

In 1763 the Spanish signed a peace treaty with the British. The former slaves at Fort Mose were shocked and upset. They refused to live again under British law, which continued to permit slavery. All the inhabitants of Fort Mose packed up and moved to Cuba, where they could once again live in freedom. The deserted fort was used for a while by the British. It finally was badly damaged during the War of 1812 (1812–1815). Over time, the remains gradually rotted and disappeared, and archaeologists found the settlement many decades later.

FREEDOM AT LAST

The original Fort Mose was the first free black town in the future United States. The people who lived there were formerly enslaved children and their families. Longing for freedom, they had bravely set out through wilderness and swamps so they could live freely in this Spanish-owned area. After the loss of the first Fort Mose, some of the residents established a second settlement with the same name twelve years later. Throughout the years in both settlements, kids and their families worked, played, and lived in the freedom they had risked their lives to earn. Fort Mose remains a symbol of the courage of these children and adults.

CONCLUSION

Kids were a vital part of all the exciting history you've read about in this book. Their labor helped the whole community as they worked side by side with adults. From drawing pictures in caves twenty thousand years ago, to crafting stone points and clay pots, to helping fish and farm, they learned traditional skills and also invented their own ways of doing things. And, in turn, they taught younger kids.

Kids all over the world, of course, did these things and others. From the reindeer hunters and herders in Scandinavia and Russia to the Maori people of New Zealand, from the kids working in the rice fields of China to the North American Inuit who wore snowshoes and rode on dogsleds, kids throughout history and around the globe had many ways of interacting with their families, environments, cultures, and religions.

In early American history, some kids were apprentices to printers, silver makers, and shipbuilders, to name a few. Other boys and girls lived in wealthy houses and played with expensive dolls, toy fiddles, toy watches, and more. And for centuries, in these same households, children living in slavery had to serve kids and adults or had to work in farm fields, straining their muscles every day.

So now that you've met some of these children from long ago, what do you think? Would you get along? Would you play and laugh and share? And what would you most want to ask these kids about their lives? One thing is for sure: kids in the past were a lot like you, but we also have a lot to learn from them!

Archaeologists search for artifacts at an excavation site in France.

AUTHOR'S NOTE

To learn more about children in the past, archaeologists often study kids' burials and the artifacts left in their graves. I chose not to do that in this book. I wanted to show what kids did when they were alive. After all, gifts left in graves were put there by adults, not by the children. They may not have had the same value to the kids who were laid to rest as they did for the adults who mourned them.

Archaeologists continue to find evidence of children of the past—sometimes the recent past! A house's yard might contain plastic toy soldiers, pick-up sticks, tiny cars, and more. And lots of our garbage is hauled away to make giant mountains of trash called landfills. Archaeologists are excavating some of these trash mountains to look at how whole communities lived—kids included.

We too are building archaeological sites every day. What will you leave behind, and what will it say about your life? Archaeologists in the future may study the digital artifacts you create, such as videos, movies, and photographs—along with physical objects you leave in the ground or in landfills. What they learn will be different from what we know about those kids in the past. Unlike kids in some parts of the world and throughout most of history, you probably don't take part in the full range of adult activities yet. Instead, you probably enjoy activities like school and play and sports. But this still prepares you for being part of your community. You learn to read and write so you can know about the world and communicate with other people. Playing with your friends, being on a sports team, or belonging to a club helps you learn how to work with others.

The scientists, historians, and archaeologists of the future will be very interested in seeing what you did with your time. So keep doing it!

SOURCE NOTES

37 William Strachey, *The Historie of Travaile into Virginia Britannia* (London: Hakluyt Society, 1849), 65.

38 Henry Spelman, "First Hand Account," *Virtual Jamestown*, accessed April 20, 2016, http://www.virtualjamestown.org/exist/cocoon/jamestown/fha/J1040.

39 Ibid.

GLOSSARY

apprentice: a student who works for and learns from a master craftsman for a period of years

caliper: an instrument used to measure the thickness or diameter of an object

chert: gray or black quartz that is usually found in limestone rock and can be chipped into a tool

coprolite: dried or fossilized poop

flint: gray or black very hard quartz that can be formed into a tool. Flint is found in Europe and in the western states of North America.

hearth: a place where a fire is lit for heat and cooking

knapper: someone who works chert or flint into tools

landfills: areas where trash from whole neighborhoods are buried

plantation: any very large farm but a term mostly applied to large farms in the southern United States

projectile point: a chert or flint tool that is fitted onto the end of a shaft for hunting and warfare

radiation: energy in the form of rays released as an object's molecules change, usually due to heat

radiocarbon dating: a method of measuring the release of radiation from objects

steatite: a soft rock, often called soapstone, that can be made into objects

thimble: a small pitted cap worn on a finger while sewing to help push the needle through fabric

venison: deer meat

SELECTED BIBLIOGRAPHY

Bagwell, Elizabeth A. "Ceramic Form and Skill." In *Children in the Prehistoric Puebloan Southwest*. Edited by Kathryn A. Kamp. Salt Lake City: University of Utah Press, 2002.

Baxter, Jane Eva. *The Archaeology of Childhood: Children, Gender, and Material Culture*. Walnut Creek, CA: AltaMira, 2005.

Bower, Bruce. "Children of Prehistory: Stone Age Kids Left Their Marks on Cave Art and Stone Tools." *Science News* 171, no. 17 (April 28, 2007): 264–265.

Deagan, Kathleen, and Darcie MacMahon. *Fort Mose, Colonial America's Black Fortress of Freedom*. Gainesville: University Press of Florida, 1995.

Harrington, J. C. *A Tryal of Glasse, the Story of Glassmaking at Jamestown*. Richmond: Dietz, 1972.

Rountree, Helen C., and E. Randolph Turner III. *Before and After Jamestown, Virginia's Powhatans and Their Predecessors*. Gainesville: University Press of Florida, 2002.

Williams, Geoff. "Mysteries of Ancient Poop." *Dig* 4, no. 4 (July/August 2002): 10–13.

FOR MORE INFORMATION

BOOKS

Curtis, Gregory. *The Cave Painters: Probing the Mysteries of the World's First Artists*. New York: Anchor Books, 2007.

Lange, Karen E. *1607: A New Look at Jamestown*. Washington, DC: National Geographic, 2007.

Turner, Glennette Tilley. *Fort Mose: And the Story of the Man Who Built the First Free Black Settlement in Colonial America*. New York: Abrams Books for Young Readers, 2010.

Walker, Sally M. *Written in Bone: Buried Lives of Jamestown and Colonial Maryland*. Minneapolis: Carolrhoda Books, 2009.

WEBSITES

Fort Mose
> http://fortmose.org
> Explore the history of the first free black settlement in the United States.

Jamestowne Rediscovery
> http://historicjamestowne.org/
> Learn about the people and history of the Jamestown settlement.

Lascaux: A Visit to the Cave
> http://www.lascaux.culture.fr/?lng=en#/en/00.xml
> Make a virtual visit to a French cave featuring a variety of magnificent ancient art.

PLACES TO VISIT

Arizona State Museum
> http://www.statemuseum.arizona.edu
> With more than twenty thousand whole vessels, Arizona State Museum has the world's largest and most comprehensively documented collection of Southwest American Indian pottery.

Art Caves of France
> http://archaeology-travel.com/thematic-guides/cave-art-in-france/
> France is home to many caves featuring prehistoric art.

Historic Jamestown, Virginia
> http://historicjamestowne.org/visit/
> Jamestown is one of the oldest settlements in the United States. It was abandoned in the late seventeenth century but has been excavated by archaeologists over many years. The current archaeological work is very exciting, as the original fort has been found. A new museum explains these findings, and the archaeological work continues nearby.

Saint Augustine, Florida
> http://augustine.com
> This is the oldest city in the United States. The original town is a tourist site with interpretations of life under the Spanish, including life at Fort Mose.

INDEX

PHOTO ACKNOWLEDGMENTS

The images in this book are used with the permission of: © AAA Photostock/Alamy, pp. 5 (top left), 47; © J Paul/Bloomberg/Getty Images, p. 5 (top right); © James Quine/Alamy, p. 5 (bottom left); © Courtesy of Roberto Ontañón Peredo and Dean Snow, p. 6; © Laura Westlund/Independent Picture Service, pp. 7, 17, 27, 33, 43; © James King-Holmes/Science Source, p. 8; © DeAgostini/Getty Images, pp. 9, 42; © KEENPRESS/National Geographic Stock, p. 10; © Age fotostock/Alamy, pp. 11, 50; © Arterra Picture Library/Alamy, p. 12; © Universal Images Group/Getty Images, p. 14; © Sutton-Hibber/Getty Images, p. 16; © De Agostini Picture Library/Getty Images, p. 18; © DEA/A. DAGLI ORTI/De Agostini/Getty Images, p. 20; © Paul D. Stewart/Science Source, p. 21; © Alinari Archives/Getty Images, p. 22; AP Photo/Jeff Barnard, p. 24; © Rosemarie Stennul/Alamy, p. 26; Photo by Joyce Heuman Kramer, courtesy of the Crow Canyon Archaeological Center, p. 28; © Don Farrall/PhotoDisc/Getty Images, p. 29; Courtesy of Texas Beyond History.net, Texas Archeological Research Laboratory, University of Texas-Austin, p. 30; © Marilyn Angel Wynn/Nativestock.com, p. 31; © MPI/Stringer/Getty Images, p. 32; © Jamestown Rediscovery, pp. 35 (all), 39; © Peter Newark American Pictures/Bridgeman Images, p. 36 (all); © Richard Cummins/Corbis Documentary/Getty Images, p. 38; © Ann Ronan Pictures/Print Collector/Getty Images, p. 44; © interfoto/Alamy, p. 48.

Front cover: © Thom Lang/Alamy.

Jacket flaps: © photostOK/REX/Shutterstock.

Back cover: © Ira Block/National Geographic/Getty Images.

ABOUT THE AUTHOR

Lois Miner Huey is an archaeologist for the State of New York. She also writes nonfiction articles and books for kids, focusing on history and archaeology. She enjoys using archaeology to determine what life was like for people who didn't leave many written records. Huey lives near Albany, New York, in a very old house with her archaeologist husband and three wonderful cats.